FOUNDATIONS OF GROWING AND LEA

How We Learn Series

Imagine you have a toy box full of different toys.

Your brain is like the toy box.

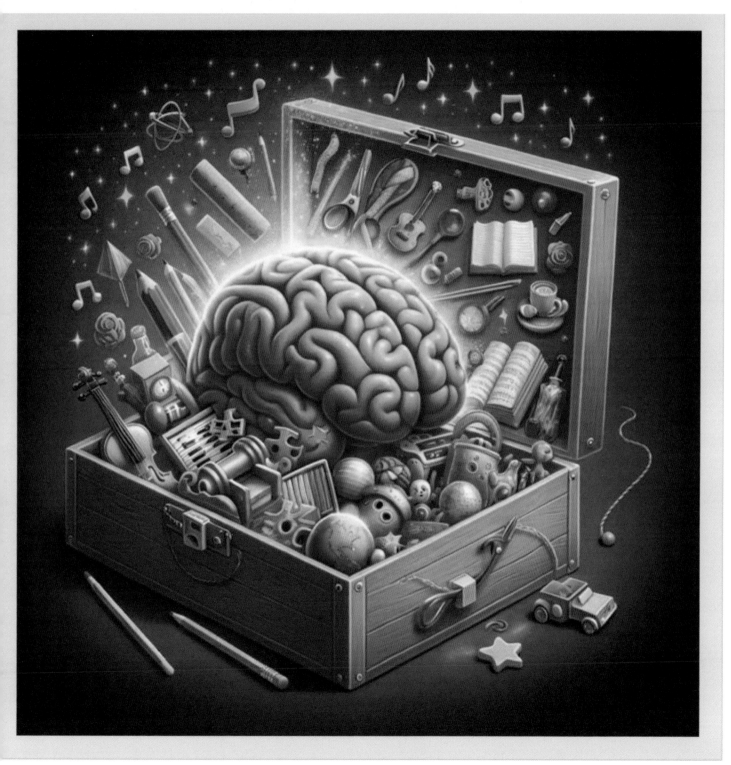

Remembering what you learned is like reaching into your brain to find that memory.

Retrieval practice is like taking out that toy from your toy box...

...except you are taking something you learned from your brain.

To learn something well you need to take it out over

and over again.

This is called practice.

Each time will get easier

and easier to retrieve
what you learned.

But you have to retrieve it all by yourself.

At first it might be hard to remember it all by yourself.

That's OK!

We get help and try again!

This is called retrieval practice. It is important for learning.

Printed in Great Britain
by Amazon